RED DOG BLUE DOG

When Pooches Get Political

CHUCK SAMBUCHINO

RUNNING PRESS
PHILADELPHIA · LONDON

© 2012 by Chuck Sambuchino
Published by Running Press,
A Member of the Perseus Books Group

*Books published by Running Press are available at special discounts for bulk purchases in
the United States by corporations, institutions, and other organizations. For more information,
please contact the Special Markets Department at the Perseus Books Group, 2300 Chestnut
Street, Suite 200, Philadelphia, PA 19103, or call (800) 810-4145, ext. 5000, or e-mail
special.markets@perseusbooks.com.*

ISBN 978-0-7624-4639-1
Library of Congress Control Number: 2012938040

E-book ISBN 978-0-7624-4711-4

9   8   7   6   5   4   3   2   1
Digit on the right indicates the number of this printing

Edited by Jennifer Leczkowski
Cover and interior design by Jason Kayser
Typography: Chronicle and Cooper Black

Running Press Book Publishers
2300 Chestnut Street
Philadelphia, PA 19103-4371

Visit us on the web!
www.runningpress.com

Milk-Bone is a trademark of Del Monte Corporation.

Dedication

This book is dedicated to my dog, Graham,
who is well on his way to being both the
world's laziest and world's flabbiest pooch.
But he does fill the world around him with love
every single day—and for that, I am a happier
person and eternally grateful.

Red Dog and Blue Dog reacted differently to news of the election results.

Introduction

If you never stopped to consider that dogs have political leanings just like we do, think again. Pooches of all sizes and breeds are constantly expressing their liberal and conservative opinions in what they bark at, what kind of music drives them into a puppy fit, and what candidates' signs they may or may not happen to pee on during that mid-afternoon walk.

The connection between dogs and politics is nothing new. In fact, a close study of the pets of our presidents reveals much about the shape of history. Franklin D. Roosevelt owned at least seven dogs, all of which were alleged to have been firmly in support of The New Deal. And as the years go on, rumor is that presidents' dogs are becoming more and more influential in having their opinions heard. It's alleged that Ronald Reagan's dog, Rex, was actually the first to champion across-the-board, sweeping tax cuts. Last year, anonymous sources say Barack Obama's new Portuguese water dog, Bo, was key in getting several bills passed. All this is to say nothing of the fact that some "unusual paw prints" were found in the Watergate Hotel in 1972, while the whereabouts of Richard Nixon's dog, Checkers, on that fateful night were never fully accounted for.

Red Dog / Blue Dog is the world's first book that offers insight into dogs' true thoughts on politics—proving that some tails wag further to the left and others to the right. In these pages, you will find canine opinions on issues such as environmental regulations, the peer pressure to compost, and the absolute fury one feels when some jerk-face steals their yard signs.

Red Dog heard your argument supporting gay marriage but still respectfully disagrees.

Blue Dog is out of the closet and doesn't care what you think.

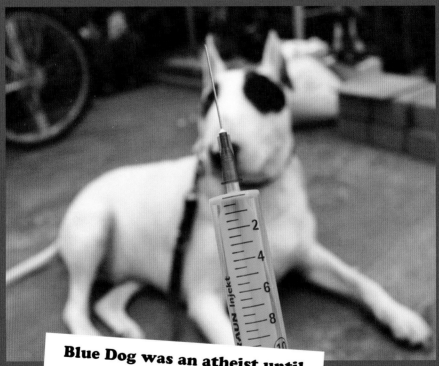

Blue Dog was an atheist until about 30 seconds ago.

Red Dog recites
the Pledge of Allegiance
and shouts the
"Under God" part.

Blue Dog enjoys reliving her flower power hippie days.

Red Dog demonstrates how a bath works for all hippies watching.

Red Dogs are getting ready to head to church.

Blue Dogs are getting ready to head to Burning Man.

Blue Dog is proud of being part of the 99 percent.

Red Dog got dragged to Occupy Wall Street and is seriously scared out of his mind.

Red Dog has read the entire Patriot Act— twice—and enjoyed every word.

Blue Dog fears Big Brother cats are listening.

Red Dog signed
up for the tea party event
but only now
realizes his error.

Blue Dog tries to draw attention to waterboarding but only now realizes her error.

Red Dog isn't so much pro-Romney as he is anti-Obama.

Blue Dog just heard
Obama's coming to town!

Blue Dog is trying to look older so he can vote.

22

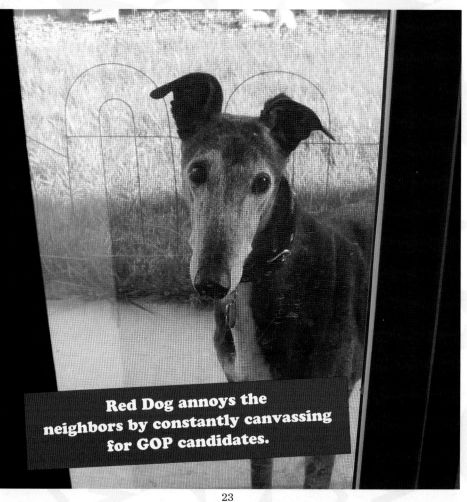

Red Dog annoys the neighbors by constantly canvassing for GOP candidates.

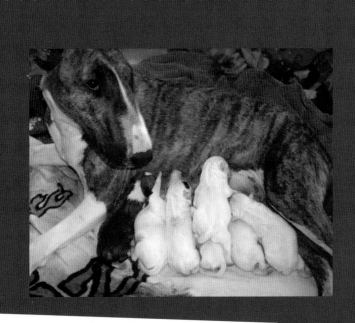

Blue Dog wonders if Social Security will be around to help her kids.

Two out of three Red Dogs agree with privatizing Social Security.

Red Dog says if you don't take off your hat for the national anthem, he will bite you in the butt.

Blue Dog is a little shaken up after a redneck guy called him a "commie moron" but is now thinking of a clever retort for later.

27

Red Dog gets fired up listening to Rush Limbaugh on his drive to work.

Blue Dog loves NPR on long car rides.

Blue Dogs think we should share everything . . .

FOR
DOGS
ONLY

. . . Red Dog disagrees.

Blue Dog won't shut up about her holistic medicine practice.

Red Dog refuses to accept patients who back Obama's healthcare plan.

Red Dog relishes pooping on the *New York Times*.

Blue Dog loves his new
e-reader because
he can get all of his liberal
media in one place.

Blue Dog is proud of cutting down on his carbon emissions.

Red Dog says his truck may guzzle gas, but damn does he look good in it.

Red Dog is confused as to what a carbon footprint is.

Blue Dog just started to compost this year and loves it.

Red Dog is ready to bag himself a 10-point buck this hunting season.

Blue Dog thinks PETA would be very interested to know about your calfskin purse.

Blue Dog thinks
the government should
make low-flow toilets
mandatory to
save the environment.

Red Dog doesn't need the government to tell him how fast he can go on his hog.

Blue Dogs believe in alternative punishment and think felons should be able to vote.

Red Dog is tough
on crime.

Blue Dog just got back from the concert and, no, he doesn't think his pupils look funny.

Red Dog looks smashing
in his opera attire.

Red Dog thinks the Fourth of July is the best holiday ever.

Blue Dog thinks Valentine's Day is a fake Hallmark holiday.

Blue Dog says if he's elected, there will be free Milk-Bones for all.

Red Dog says, "Read my hips—
no new taxes!"

Red Dog votes a straight GOP ticket and is incredibly partisan . . .

. . . but not as partisan as Blue Dog.

**Blue Dog reminds you that
we were all immigrants at one time.**

Red Dogs finally got that border fence built.

Blue Dog just tried some wild 'shrooms on a dare and is totally wigging out.

Red Dog thinks you're hanging out with the wrong crowd.

Blue Dog thinks politicians should compromise and meet in the middle.

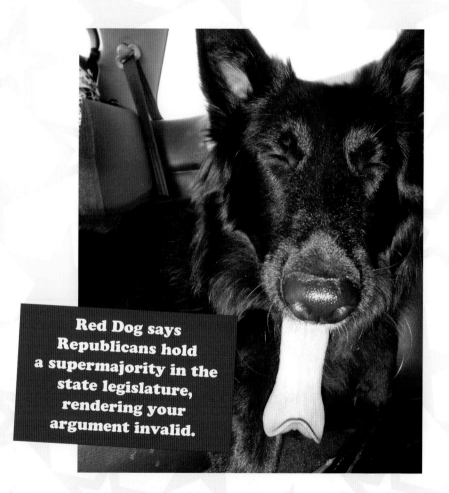

Red Dog says Republicans hold a supermajority in the state legislature, rendering your argument invalid.

Blue Dog tries to raise awareness about the melting polar ice caps.

Red Dog thinks the whole global
warming thing is a crock.

Blue Dog regrets his crossover vote.

Red Dog regrets his crossover vote.

Red Dog cannot help but dry heave every time he sees Nancy Pelosi on TV.

Blue Dog gets like this when you put on Fox News.

Red Dog yearns for simpler times, better-made automobiles, and snazzier outfits.

Blue Dogs just want to
legalize it already.

Blue Dog has the sunrise in his Facebook profile pic to show you he's sensitive.

Red Dog doesn't take kindly to strangers 'round these parts.

Red Dog has not yet successfully destroyed all old Mardi Gras photos.

Blue Dog can neither confirm nor deny that this photo on Twitter is actually her.

71

Red Dog is ready to play the national anthem at the Indy 500.

Blue Dog is happy to play
some Springsteen
by request.

Blue Dog just learned they raised taxes on the super rich.

Red Dog just learned he's in a higher tax bracket this year.

75

Red Dog still uses the same landline he installed back in the day.

Blue Dog would tell you stories about back in the day if he could remember them.

Red Dog wants a
tax break for Christmas.

Blue Dog got what he wanted for Christmas: 52 miles to the gallon.

Blue Dog says UNION YES.

Red Dog believes in fair wages for honest work.

Red Dog says these colors don't bleed.

Blue Dog says these don't either.

Red Dog thinks only
God could make a
scene this beautiful
and is quick to tell anyone
who walks by.

Blue Dog successfully
sued to have the
10 Commandments taken out
of the courthouse.

Blue Dog loves his new ranch but wishes he weren't the only Democrat in the entire county.

Red Dog says them city folk just don't know what they're missin'.

Red Dog would like to know why these flags were made in China.

Blue Dog would like to know if
this dog bone is organic and fair-trade.

Red Dog doesn't mind some mudslinging come election time.

Blue Dog calls you out in public when you're not politically correct.

Blue Dog thinks your police state is fascist.

Red Dog says love it or leave it.

Red Dog must have his brandy and smoking jacket in the evening.

Blue Dog thinks his Red Dog uncle looks ridiculous in that jacket.

Blue Dog supports legalizing interspecies marriage.

Red Dog has nightmares about activist judges.

97

Blue Dog always ruins beach days by bringing up the BP oil spill.

Red Dog
always ruins trips
to the museums
by bringing
up creationism.

Red Dog would like to see your long-form birth certificate.

Blue Dog thinks your flat tax plan is preposterous.

Blue Dog is an outspoken liberal who never misses a Maureen Dowd column.

Red Dog is proud of being a Republican, if you couldn't tell.

103

Red Dog is on the NASCAR bandwagon after Danica Patrick signed up.

Blue Dog is on the vegan bandwagon after Bill Clinton jumped on.

Red Dog saw Ted Nugent
do this once.

106

Blue Dog guilts you into recycling this bottle and can.

Blue Dogs moved to Canada to protest Bush's re-election.

Red Dog refuses to
get out of bed until Obama is
no longer in office.

Blue Dogs listen reverently to Obama's State of the Union.

Red Dog doesn't want to hear another word.

Red Dog enjoys his time in the great wide open.

Blue Dog spends
way too much time doing
nothing in his tiny
Manhattan apartment.

Blue Dog just decided he wants to be cremated because it's more ecologically responsible.

Red Dog says to bury him with his Texas hat on when he dies.

115

Blue Dog says if you want to cut down this tree, you'll have to get through her first.

Red Dog cut down all the trees on his land.

Blue Dog can't help but think how perfect the world would have been if Gore won.

Red Dog is getting really pissed at whoever keeps stealing his Ron Paul yard signs.

Blue Dog waits patiently for the government to plow her street.

Red Dog don't need no stinkin' government.

Red Dog says,
"I am not a crook!"

Blue Dog says, "It depends on what the definition of 'is' is."

Red Dog is focused
on balancing the budget.

Blue Dog is focused on balancing the biscuits.

Red Dog is so patriotic and cute that you forget she's a right-wing nut job.

Blue Dog is good
at calligraphy and Scrabble,
but besides that is
just an insufferable bore.

127

Blue Dog considers herself a DIY locavore.

Red Dog is sure it tastes better when someone else is serving it.

Red Dog has a one-thirty tee time with the district attorney.

**Blue Dogs wonder
who has time for golf when
you have the open road.**

Red Dog tells his friends, "My wife thinks I'm on a work trip. BEER ME!"

When Blue Dog is away, he checks in
with his wife every two hours.

Red Dog wishes his doctor spoke English.

Blue Dog is just fine with universal healthcare.

Blue Dog believes in euthanasia.

Red Dog feels all life is precious.

Blue Dogs remind you of the first Thanksgiving and the carnage that came after it.

Red Dog always says
"Merry Christmas"
and never
"Happy Holidays."

Red Dogs patrol the Florida coastline and send illegals back to Cuba...

... but they didn't catch them all.

Photo Credits

Cover (red dog): ©Shutterstock.com/Dannay
Cover (blue dog): ©Shutterstock.com/AISPIX
    by Image Source
Back cover: ©iStockphoto.com/Sharon Dominick

4:    ©Marianna Ahearn
6:    ©William Shunn & Laura Chavoen
7:    ©Laurie Cutter
8:    ©Saskia Liebscher
9:    ©Katherine Cummins
10:    ©Pat Caporali
11:    ©Pat Caporali
12:    ©Cassandra Marshall
13:    ©Todd Colby Pliss
14:    ©Drew Mokris
15:    ©Bridget Rhee
16:    ©Jim Merk
17:    ©Aimee Loiselle
18:    ©Chelsea Ann Redinger
19:    ©Cari Sultanik
20:    ©Sylvia Labelle
21:    ©Joi Lasnick
22:    ©Joi Lasnick
23:    ©Mike Chen
24:    ©Sherrie Seymour
25:    ©Karen Martinac
26:    ©Angela Harger
27:    ©Marley S. Diehl
28:    ©Roberta F. King
29:    ©Chandra Perkins
30:    ©Sharron Kahn Luttrell
31:    ©William Shunn & Laura Chavoen
32:    ©Michele Yoo
33:    ©Zachary Petit
34:    ©Zachary Petit

35:    ©Genevieve Petrillo
36:    ©Cristian Vargas
37:    ©Sylvia Labelle
38:    ©Sylvia Labelle
39:    ©Barbara Youree
40:    ©Gregory M. Query
41:    ©Michele Yoo
42:    ©Lisa Harris
43:    ©Anna L. LeBlanc
44:    ©Jessica Lee Anderson
45:    ©Ingrid Hansen Smythe
46:    ©Liz Crain
47:    ©Janine Kahn
48:    ©Jennet Agus
49:    ©Sharron Kahn Luttrell
50:    ©David Jennings
51:    ©Reed Braden
52:    ©Brian Stucki
53:    ©Jill Beninato & Sit Stay Smile
    Photography
54:    ©Angelica
55:    ©Connie Soper
56:    ©Debbie Hendrickx
57:    ©Debbie Hendrickx
58:    ©Sylvia Labelle
59:    ©Erinne Sevigny
60:    ©Chuck Sambuchino
61:    ©Peter M. Roarke
62:    ©Su Williams
63:    ©Diane Masi
64:    ©Chuck Sambuchino & Graham the Dog
65:    ©Kathryn Elizabeth Brown
66:    ©Betty Aragon-Mitotes
67:    ©Mimi Ditchie
68:    ©Saskia Liebscher

69: ©Laurie Cutter
70: ©Linda R. Stollar
71: ©Tasha M. Edmonds
72: ©Debbie Hendrickx
73: ©Susan Boucher
74: ©Veronica Robertson
75: ©Sean and Frances Yates
76: ©Zachary Petit
77: ©Nancy Dontigney
78: ©Erin James
79: ©Nancy Boyce
80: ©Elisabeth Kinsey
81: ©Zachary Petit
82: ©Chas Dye
83: ©Lulu Hoeller
84: ©Angelica
85: ©Sylvia Labelle
86: ©LuAnne DeMeo Jackson
87: ©Gregory M. Query
88: ©Michele Keesser
89: ©Es Goodman
90: ©Connie Soper
91: ©David Jones
92: ©Mary Witter
93: ©Laura Lok
94: ©Zachary Petit
95: ©Renea L. Dahms
96: ©Diane Masi
97: ©Zachary Petit
98: ©Pat Caporali
99: ©Layne Runyon
100: ©Robert Tamburo
101: ©Danielle Brochner
102: ©Carol J. Bro
103: ©Jennifer Duncan Dole
104: ©Myles Lee Crampton
105: ©Jayn Lando

106: ©Brandy Lawrence
107: ©Zachary Petit
108: ©Sylvia Labelle
109: ©Sean Gowdy
110: ©Veronica Robertson
111: ©Cassandra Parrish
112: ©Peter M. Roarke
113: ©Joe Aurelio
114: ©Chuck Sambuchino & Graham the Dog
115: ©LuAnne DeMeo Jackson
116: ©Jeanne Pursell
117: ©Sylvia Labelle
118: ©Sylvia Labelle
119: ©Allison Hart
120: ©Pat Caporali
121: ©Jessica Morelock
122: ©Christina Ruotolo
123: ©LuAnne DeMeo Jackson
124: ©LuAnne DeMeo Jackson
125: ©Rosalyn Acero & Golden Woofs
126: ©Lauren Ott
127: ©Bryan Yen
128: ©Sharron Kahn Luttrell
129: ©LuAnne DeMeo Jackson
130: ©Gregory M. Query
131: ©Patty Scott Smith
132: ©Gregory M. Query
133: ©Amy O Pry & Dogtired Ranch Small Dog Rescue
134: ©Kristan Hoffman
135: ©John Hallam
136: ©Stacey and Mark Narduzzi
137: ©Joan Ranquet
138: ©Kimberly Stephens
139: ©Joe Aurelio
140: ©Angelica
141: ©Melissa Stewart

Acknowledgments

Three women had a huge role in bringing this book to life. The first person to thank, always, is my wife Bre, whose support of my work is amazing. She helped me come up with the idea, and was also the one who forced me, practically at gunpoint, to get a dog in 2008. Secondly, my agent Sorche Fairbank worked very hard to see this book come to life. Lastly, my editor, Jen Leczkowski, believed in this idea from the beginning and was its champion. To all three women, I say thank you.

The next people to thank are all the amazing photographers, amateur and professional, who contributed images to this zany project. There is no way this book would exist without the help and contributions of hundreds of people I contacted through Flickr, Twitter, and Facebook. (Take note, other writers: This book is a testament to the power of social media.) To everyone who submitted images—even those whose pictures did not end up in the final edits—I say thank you.

Writer's Digest staffer Zachary Petit did an amazing job with his special photography contributions, working on a very tight schedule. My sister and husband-in-law, Mary Kay and Ethan, provided excellent photo punchlines throughout the process, as did my good friend Brian A. Klems. I want to thank my book designer, Jason Kayser, for doing an amazing job bringing all these images to life. My father-in-law, Morris, was a great help with jokes. And naturally, I always give a shout-out to my parents, as well as my close friend, Tom. To all of you who helped me complete this project, I say thank you.

And lastly to Graham, my fitness-challenged dog with the body composition of a rubber chicken. All these years, I've made passive-aggressive comments at him about "eating us out of house and home" and "not contributing anything whatsoever to the household," when—wouldn't you know it—he would be the key inspiration for this book you hold in your hands. The fact that Graham proceeded to demand "double treats—forever" after hearing about this project makes me love him all the more.

To all persons I listed, and to anyone I forgot to name, I say *thank you*.